RELIGIONS OF THE WORLD

I Am a Latter-day Saint (Mormon)

❧ GAYLA WISE ❧

The Rosen Publishing Group's
PowerKids Press™
New York

Published in 1999 by The Rosen Publishing Group, Inc.
29 East 21st Street, New York, NY 10010

First Edition

Book Design: Kim Sonsky and Erin McKenna

Photo Credits and Photo Illustrations: Cover, pp. 4, 11, 15, 16, 19 by Mark Philbrick; pp. 7, 8, © Corbis-Bettmann; p. 12 © The Church of Jesus Christ of Latter-day Saints; p. 20 © Claudia Dhimitri.

Wise, Gayla.
    I am a Latter-day Saint / Gayla Wise.
        p.   cm.— (Religions of the World)
    Includes index.
    Summary: A young member of the Church of Jesus Christ of Latter-Day Saints explains the beliefs and practices of his religion.
    ISBN 0-8239-5259-2
    1. Church of Jesus Christ of Latter-Day Saints—Juvenile literature. 2. Mormon Church—Juvenile literature.
[1. Church of Jesus Christ of Latter-Day Saints. 2. Mormon Church.]
    I. Title. II. Series: Religions of the world (Rosen Publishing Group)
BX8635.2.W595 1997
289.3'32—dc21

                                                            97-32956
                                                               CIP
                                                                AC

Manufactured in the United States of America

Contents

I Am a Latter-day Saint

My name is Scott. I live near Salt Lake City, Utah. I am a member of the Church of Jesus Christ of Latter-day Saints. Sometimes I say I am LDS or Mormon. Both of these names are nicknames for my religion.

Latter-day Saints live in nearly every country of the world. Members everywhere believe the same teachings. I can go to my church anywhere in the world and hear the same lessons. A local church group is called a ward. My family belongs to a ward.

Many different kinds of families and people belong to the Church of Jesus Christ of Latter-day Saints.

Jesus Christ

We believe that there is a God. He is our Father, and Jesus Christ is God's son. God and Jesus and the Holy Ghost are three separate beings. Latter-day Saints believe that Jesus died for us to save us from **sin** (SIN) and death. He is the **Savior** (SAYV-yor) of the world. To live with Christ after we die, we must **repent** (re-PENT). Every day I pray to our Heavenly Father, or God. I end my prayers in the name of Jesus Christ. I try to be kind like Jesus.

This painting shows what some people believe God looks like. ▶

Prophets and Apostles

We believe God called a man named Joseph Smith to be a **prophet** (PRAH-fet). Through this prophet, Jesus set up his church on Earth. The president of the Church today is Gordon B. Hinckley. He is also a prophet. Through prayer, Jesus helps him to lead the church. Twelve **apostles** (uh-POS-ulz) also help him. They travel around the world teaching about Jesus Christ. Twice a year I see the prophet and apostles on TV. They speak at a meeting in Salt Lake City. Through TV, people all over the world can hear these meetings in their own languages.

◀ Mormons believe that Joseph Smith was chosen by Jesus to set up his church for other people.

Scriptures

The **scriptures** (SKRIP-cherz) are holy writings that are important to us. They teach us about God's laws. One scripture is the Bible. The Bible tells about the life, teachings, and **resurrection** (rez-er-EK-shun) of Jesus. Another scripture is the Book of Mormon. It tells the story of people living in the Americas long ago. My favorite part of the Book of Mormon is when Jesus visits the people of the Americas right after his death and resurrection. My family reads a chapter from the scriptures every night at bedtime.

The scriptures help Latter-day Saints ▶ learn more about their religion.

Baptism

Children in the Church of Jesus Christ of Latter-day Saints are **baptized** (BAP-tyzd) when they are eight years old. My dad baptized me. He could baptize me because he has the **priesthood** (PREEST-hood). Baptism is a two-way promise between God and the person being baptized. The person promises to obey God's laws. God promises to forgive, or wash away, the things we have done wrong. This is why my dad baptized me by gently laying me underwater and quickly bringing me up.

◀ Through baptism, a Latter-day Saint repents and comes out of the water to a clean, new life.

13

Sacrament

Every Sunday I go with my family to a **Sacrament** (SAK-ruh-ment) Meeting. Members of the ward give talks. But first and most importantly, we take the sacrament. We each eat a little piece of bread and drink a little cup of water. The broken bread and water remind us that Jesus died for us. We also remember the promises we made at baptism. When I turn twelve, I can be **ordained** (or-DAYND) a **deacon** (DEE-kun). Then I can pass the sacrament to other church members. When I turn sixteen, I can be ordained a priest. Then I can bless the sacrament.

During Sacrament Meeting, a deacon passes the sacrament to other church members. ▶

Primary

After Sacrament Meeting, I go with my brother and sister to **Primary** (PRY-mayr-ee). We learn the teachings of the church in our Primary classes. We have sharing time, where we talk about our beliefs. We also sing in Primary. I like singing time because my mom is the song leader. My favorite song is called "I Am a Child of God."

◀ Stories about Jesus Christ are often told in Primary.

Missionaries

Many young men and women go on **missions** (MISH-unz) for our church. Missionaries are sent all over the world. My Aunt Julie is a missionary in the country of Bolivia. She teaches people in Spanish about our beliefs in Christ. She helps them get ready for their baptisms. She also teaches them about different medicines so they won't get sick. I am saving my money so I can go on a mission someday too.

The people in this picture learned new things from missionaries who visited their country. ▶

Temples

Temples (TEM-pulz) are special buildings used for special **ceremonies** (SER-eh-mohn-eez). Latter-day Saint adults must follow God's laws to go there. My parents were married in a temple. They were **sealed** (SEELD) together for this life and for **eternity** (ee-TER-nih-tee). This means they are joined as husband and wife now and also after they die. I am sealed to my parents as their child through their temple marriage. Through this sealing, we will be a family forever.

◀ This Mormon temple is located in Salt Lake City, Utah.

Family Home Evening

Monday night is a special time for my family. We call it Family Home Evening. Each of us takes turns preparing a lesson. Sometimes we do fun things. But mostly I like being with my family and doing things together. Our family time ends, just like every other night, with a family prayer. Being a Latter-day Saint is important to me and my family. It is an important part of our lives. I learn how to live and be happy as a member of the Church of Jesus Christ of Latter-day Saints.

Glossary

Meanings given here apply to the Church of Jesus Christ of Latter-day Saints.
Some words may have different meanings in other religions.

apostle (uh-POS-ul) One of twelve men called to lead the church.

baptism (BAP-tizm) A ceremony for washing away sins with
 water and becoming a member of the church.

ceremony (SER-eh-mohn-ee) A set way to make religious promises.

deacon (DEE-kun) A position held in the priesthood.

eternity (ee-TER-nih-tee) Forever.

mission (MISH-un) When someone is sent to do special work.

ordain (or-DAYN) To give someone a position in the priesthood.

priesthood (PREEST-hood) The authority to act for God in a church
 service.

Primary (PRY-mayr-ee) A church meeting for Latter-day Saint children.

prophet (PRAH-fet) A man to whom God speaks.

repent (re-PENT) To feel sorry for doing something wrong, and to ask for
 forgiveness.

resurrection (rez-ur-EK-shun) Coming back to life after dying, and never
 dying again.

sacrament (SAK-ruh-ment) The bread and water used in some religious
 services.

Savior (SAYV-yor) Jesus Christ.

scripture (SKRIP-cher) A holy writing.

sealed (SEELD) When families are joined together forever.

sin (SIN) Breaking the laws of God on purpose.

temple (TEM-pul) A place where special religious ceremonies are
 held.

Index